Many blessings!

[signature] Sep 20

A Medium's Memoir

෫෮ ෬ය

MEAGHAN O'LEARY, PHD

The stories in this book are true. What is also true: names and other personal identifiers have been changed to preserve anonymity and certain characters, events, and timelines are composites.

For Jim

1945–2018

You knew what it meant.

For that, and everything else, my love and eternal thanks.

Acknowledgements

Throughout the extended branches of my family tree run rich veins of creative expression and spiritual seeking. Many of us are writers, poets, artists, healers, and intuitives. I am blessed to walk with all of you on this incredible journey. I love you.

To the spirit guides, ancestors, and medicine allies: thankfully you see my heart and know the depth of my gratitude for your presence in my life. May our work together serve the highest good.

Thank you, Great Mystery, for this day.

‍ॐ‍

Your life story is a gift.
Every inspiration you have ever acted upon,
anytime you have fallen in love or fallen down,
every blessing,
every curse,
every tear that has rolled down your cheek,
and every "I love you" that has crossed your lips.
Each of these things, and everything else,
has been unfailingly and generously placed upon the
Universal altar for the rest of us to receive.
For we are eternally connected.
Your pain is our pain,
your joy is our joy.
We are One.
Thank you.

‍ॐ‍

Introduction

How you live your life enables each one of us to consider the Universe from a completely fresh viewpoint. Every choice you make moves us all forward and deeper into the great mystery of existence that we share. Because of this, we are lovingly reminded that our individual interpretation of The Truth is merely a single star glimmering in a sky full of infinite truths: yours, mine, and ours. There is no single truth out there, except Love. So, on behalf of everyone, thank you, with all my heart. You are a unique, never-to-be-replicated, miracle of creation. This I know about you, one hundred percent.

And how am I so sure?

Because I am psychic.

Professionally, my practice is healing and intuitive arts. For the past eighteen years, it has been my job to remind you of your story when you forget, or when you lose faith, or when you have come to mistakenly believe in the illusion of any explanation other than that you are, indeed, *miraculous.*

Now, miraculous doesn't mean perfect. There is a big difference. Perfect means we are endlessly racing to cross a finish line that doesn't exist. Determined yet exhausted, many of us choose this path. Unconsciously (and sometimes consciously), we merge into the melee, usually following our parents, teachers, friends, and partners. We believe that if we just keep trying, doing, and striving we might, once and for all, make it—and make it right.

Miraculous doesn't always mean good or right, either; at least at first glance. Some of us live stories that veer into improbable and inexplicable territory, revealing a dark side of unconscious (and conscious) choice. Together, we create a multifaceted composition made deeper and richer by this range of contrast. Just like an artist's painting, the highlights would not shine so brightly on the canvas if not for their juxtaposition with the shadows.

If we can sit with both the shadow and the light without running away, and with deep love in our hearts, we may come to realize that neither is right or wrong, and both are needed. They are not opposites so much as two parts of a whole—each reflecting what the other is missing. If we are interested in exploring The Truth, we must be willing to look at *all* our truths. And we must be able to see the light and dark in ourselves as much as we see it in others.

If I have learned anything over the course of more than ten thousand client sessions, it is this: understanding that our life story is a gift and choosing to fully inhabit our Miraculous Self (the shadow *and* the light) is a quantum leap into a whole other realm of existence. This is an entirely different understanding about our place in the Universe and the powers of creation that are available to us. In every single moment we get to choose whether we embrace this miracle or abandon it.

I say that being psychic is my job; however, it is so much more than that. It is a true calling. Conventional definitions describe a calling as an undeniable inner conviction toward a distinct action, typically including some form of transcendent urgency. For me, it is simply that I don't know how *not* to do or *be* this. It is the life story I place on the altar, and I pray every day that it serves.

This book is a collection of my stories . . . and yours. Over the years, I have listened, witnessed, and learned. By answering Spirit's call, I am allowed to gently hold your soul story in my hands for a bit of time, sharing what I see, hear, feel, and know. The beauty of this blessing shines like a star, bringing tears of love and appreciation to my eyes.

Part I

The Dawning

ഌ൙ഌ

Chapter One

*G*reat. *I'm blind.*

It was hot. The morning sun baked my body through the scratchy fabric of the straitjacket. Every night they trussed me up in this thing out of concern for my well-being. I was getting used to being encased from collar to toes, almost like a mummy. I appreciated their loving care and attention, even though the extra protection seemed extreme and felt like it wasn't really necessary. I wished I could tell them so, yet I knew it would be a little while longer before my vocabulary extended beyond crying and laughing. *Patience is always required when starting over,* I recalled.

Really, though? I have to be blind now?

Undeterred by the confining fabric, not to mention a

newly discovered lack of sight, my legs had no problem whatsoever getting my body to stand upright against the narrow wooden bars. Their strong muscles twitched with an overpowering impulse to kick and jump. Without warning, my knees suddenly dropped down and then exploded upward like tightly coiled springs. Up and down, up and down, I rocketed higher each time. Oxygen rushed in and out of my lungs, igniting a symphony of physical chain reactions making these movements possible. Forgetting everything else for a few moments, I succumbed to the sheer joy of being alive. I marveled at the utter brilliance of this body's design and the miracle of being human.

And so, I thought, *I am to be blind too.*

"Meaghan." A clear, strong voice spoke directly into my left ear.

Instantly my body jammed on the brakes, halting every movement except for my rapid breathing and pounding heart. I swallowed hard, now on high alert. Cautiously, I turned my head toward the voice. No one was supposed to be in the room with me.

"Meaghan, listen."

I realized the voice was inexplicably coming from outside my body and inside my head all at once, like some kind of multisensory, stereophonic sound system.

What? I called out, inside my head. My face tightened into a scowl.

"Meaghan, open your eyes."

Open my eyes?

"Open your eyes!"

Of course! In this place, you must open your eyes to see. Relief washed over me like a breaking wave as I slowly opened my sleep-filled eyelids. The morning sunlight danced and flickered across the walls of my new home and rippled through the wooden bars surrounding me. I looked down to see soft baby hands gripping the smooth and sturdy top railing of a crib. My hands! My crib! Delighted, I examined further. Yep, there it was, the fuzzy yellow second skin that apparently was vital for my nighttime survival. Mom and Dad called them my "jammies." To me, they would always feel like a straitjacket.

You still here? I asked mentally.

"Still here, always here."

Smiling, I intuitively knew the comforting voice would still be there. From somewhere deep inside my awareness I remembered that nobody comes here alone—not me, not you. Everybody has a support team of guardian angels, spirit guides, allies, or ancestors; they go by different names depending on your belief system. They are here, assisting, even if you do not believe in them or have forgotten they exist.

Feeling renewed now that the morning's mystery was quickly and easily resolved by remembering to open my eyes, my body started jumping up and down again, instinctively, exuberantly, as if taking flight.

I am ready for this life!

"Yes, you are." The voice laughed warmly.

ℬ ℭ

That was my very first memory. Where it all began, as far as I can remember. Our home was remodeled shortly after I was born, so my crib was moved out of a second-story bedroom to the landing adjacent to the stairway. This temporary placement positioned me directly beneath a large double-hanging window facing east. Picture an ant under a magnifying glass that has been perfectly angled to intensify the morning sun's rays and you get the idea. This was the 1960s, so I was suited up for bed in a cloth diaper, plastic pants, and full-body, footed pajamas that zipped up to the neck and was secured, noose-like, with a flap that snapped over the zipper's pull tab. Comparing this getup to a strait-jacket was not an overstatement.

When you consider some of your own earliest memories for a moment, have you ever stopped to wonder how you made it through alive? Is it really all that surprising that we are in need of some help down here? Without our nonphysical support team (our spirit guides) acting as navigators, all of us would be flying blind, so to speak. I imagine, early in the development of humankind on this planet, it quickly became apparent that this earth story wasn't going to last very long without some outside assistance. With some well-planned divine intervention, our friends in the other realm have been making it a point to help us ever since.

Childhood, my guides tell me—particularly the early years—is an important phase of soul integration. We have left our home in the spirit world and have temporarily returned to this beautiful planet as a physical body. This concept—called reincarnation or "entering the flesh again" (which is the literal meaning of the word)—is a principle of many world religions and philosophies. Even though most of us can find the exact time of our birth typed on a legal certificate, launching a life isn't quite as precise as activating a stopwatch. It is more like making salad dressing by mixing oil and vinegar together. It is an emulsification in which two separate states of being (soul and body) interface to form a cohesive partnership.

Like all partnerships, there is an inherent instability within—a little bit of tension between remaining in the new state and returning to the original. Over time, however, the commitment and desire to stay in the new life softens this tension, or at least allows it to lie dormant much of the time. Mostly this happens thanks to the distractions and discoveries of day-to-day living in a brand-new human body. However, sometimes the edges blur and we once again become aware of the other side and those who watch over us, just as I did that long-ago morning waking up in my crib. Just as you have been aware of being helped by something or someone you just can't explain—when you let yourself remember.

Chapter Two

Christmastime in my early childhood home was twenty-four carat magic, and all the credit for this goes to my mother. As soon as Thanksgiving was over, our home would begin that unmistakable rumbling and humming. I could sense it, the way I imagine an aspen tree does when it's time to let go the leaves from its branches. It was a time of excited anticipation and I walked around with a perpetual case of butterflies in my stomach that made it nearly impossible to sleep.

With turkey leftovers barely cool in the fridge, my mom expertly waved her decorating wand and our home exploded into a multisensory holiday story land. It was the same every year and I loved it, especially the Christmas tree. Even now, I'll go to almost any length to bury my nose in fresh evergreen boughs, including crossing a neighbor's fence. That smell! My big sister is the same way. Like foxhounds, we will stop dead in our tracks and follow any scent evoking childhood memories, from flowering tulip trees to Sunday roast dinner. Growing up in Idaho, our Christmas tree was always a freshly cut noble fir beauty, and it was always huge. Not only huge to me because I was a small kid, no; this tree would top my dad by a good three feet, probably more.

I was utterly enchanted with the beauty of Christmas while at the same time curious about the science involved. What, exactly, was the magic behind those hundreds of twinkling lights snaking up the tree? I knew the glowing red holly berries that clustered around a twisted green electrical cord weren't really *real*, although I considered popping one into my mouth to make sure. However, since I had learned that using my mouth to investigate random items often resulted in an unpleasant trip to the family doctor, I decided against it.

Looking for answers, I pried open the plastic panes of "stained glass" that formed a string of small jewel-toned lanterns, making sure the flickering flame inside wasn't actually on fire (it wasn't; I was disappointed, though not really surprised). Scooching back from the giant tree to rest and reconsider, my eyes fell to the several inches of barely visible brown trunk that disappeared into a Christmas-colored cloud of skirting fabric. That's when I noticed a single cord hanging in the shadows under the tree. I followed its path as it ran along one wall, turned a corner, and ran along the next, finally stopping at the mouth of an electrical outlet. *Ah-ha,* I nodded to myself, thinking, *I know about these things, they're called "plug-ins."*

This must be the solution to the mystery of the Christmas lights! The answers to all my questions would surely be inside one of the little slots in that outlet. Hunkered down on the soft carpeting, I resolved to get a close-up look at things and unplugged the cord from the wall. Tilting my face sideways, with one eye narrowed almost shut and the other bug-eyed, I focused in on the cover plate like it was a microscope. And . . .

Nothing.

All the prong holes were too tiny and too dark to see anything inside of them.

Well then, enough of this! I thought. I looked down at my hands. My fingers might be small enough, especially the pinkie. Without any hesitation, I jammed my tiniest finger right into one of those little holes. It didn't go in very far— but it turns out, it went in just far enough. With odds being equal, I had managed to choose one of the prong holes dedicated to delivering the "hot" electrical current, straight from the breaker box. There were two things I couldn't have known at the time: electricity will always choose the fastest and most direct path to the ground, and the human body is an excellent conductor for this journey, particularly when proffered by the gooey, candy cane-stained fingertip of a four-year-old.

Boom. And then . . .

"Meaghan."

Oh boy, here we go again. The voice is back, I thought to myself.

"Meaghan."

Yep, I'm here, I said silently.

Or was I? Something was different; I felt strange, like I was dreaming and awake all at once. I also felt somehow removed from my surroundings. Gazing around, our house looked the same, yet everything appeared made up, like the furniture in my dollhouse. I was also inexplicably standing on the opposite side of our large living room, far away from the Christmas lights and the outlet. I glanced back in that direction and saw that there was a body lying on the floor.

My body!

"Yes, that is your body." The voice said.

By this time in my life, the visiting voice had become familiar. He always spoke with a calm, reassuring tone. I didn't hear him with my ears, exactly; it was as if I heard him through the side of my head. This ability to communicate without using my ears or mouth was becoming as natural to me as breathing, even though it would be years before I learned to call this skill "telepathy." Together, our information exchanges included language, feelings, and attitudes simultaneously. His mental words, though simple and direct, had always been imparted with affectionate patience and undertones of gentle humor. I knew instinctively that I could trust him.

Am I asleep? I wondered, still looking at my motionless body lying across the room. In my mind, I turned to the voice. *What happened to me?*

"I caught you. It was like a little explosion that knocked you outside of your body."

Huh, I thought, still trying to make sense of the last few moments. *Well, it didn't hurt.*

"No. It happened very fast."

I like it here with you. I feel good. And I did. I felt light, peaceful, and so relaxed, as if this moment could last forever. Becoming curious, I started to imagine all the things I could do in this state. Maybe I could sneak out to the snow-covered backyard without a coat, maybe even without shoes. I'd just see if anyone noticed, and if no one did, well, then it was a short sprint to the back gate and I'd be off to anywhere in the neighborhood I liked. Being without a body could very well turn out to have distinct advantages.

"Meaghan, you are going to wake up in a minute or two and you will be back over there, back inside your body."

Snapping out of my fantasy as a newly invisible superhero, I turned. *Wait. What? How come?*

"Because that is where you really want to be right now. You know this."

I opened my mouth to debate, then realized I really did want to go back and wake up. I could feel an ache in my chest, and I started missing my mom and dad. I was even missing my big sister. Suddenly, I wanted more than anything for things to go back to the way they had been just minutes earlier. I wanted to hear the familiar and comforting sounds emanating from other rooms in the house. I wanted that more than anything else in the world.

And, just like that, I was back.

The transition into my physical body was startling. A moment ago, as a being of light, I was energetically agile, able to move at the speed of thought. Now my body felt heavy and cumbersome, like it was solidifying in amber resin. I was happy and relieved, though. It had been a close call and I knew it.

As I sat up, I shook my hand in an attempt to bring feeling back to my fingers. I was thirsty and my mouth felt dusty. I sat for a few minutes, remembering the Christmas tree lights and my adventure to discover the origin of their twinkling magic. Well, now I knew. Electrical outlets are for the stuff you want to do things with, like when it's time to vacuum the carpet or when I want to listen to the record player. They are not for sticking your fingers into. Check.

To this day, I insert electrical plugs into their sockets

with my fingers positioned a good inch back from the prongs. I'm not taking any chances.

∞ ∞

When it's your time, it's your time. And when it's not, it's not. And, no, this is not just some feel-good platitude to make you more comfortable about death. I've seen it. Or rather, I have been shown this multiple times, both in client sessions and in my own life.

There is an underlying divine Universal order to all things. The timing of your transition—your crossing over— is determined with precision and intention. Beings of spirit begin assembling around you prior to your departure time. Their purpose is to help activate the energies, intersections, choices, and actions that culminate in your passage to the other side. Then, like midwives, they support the natural process that we humans often complicate through resistance, assumptions, or fear.

Dying is quite easy—the actual undertaking of it, that is. The physical body is programmed to let go of life by shutting down the millions of functions it had been handling, smoothly and without notice, for your entire lifetime. The heart center leads this effort, as it is the midway point between this life and the afterlife. It is the heart that begins the physical and energetic shifts that bring about the necessary chain of reactions that allow the soul to depart from the physical body.

Death itself feels quite pleasant—warm and expansive. The mind frees itself from the confines of the human brain and psyche. The ego reconstitutes itself into its native state as an energetic organ of connectivity. You regain the knowledge that you are just one aspect of an entire dynamic system. What our spiritual teachers say is true: we are literally all one. You will return to this oneness much like a single drop of mercury migrates to unite with a larger pool of mercury.

The souls who wish to stay connected with those still living may opt to do so. They may discover their mission is to continue serving through their physical earth persona, which they can continue to use when interacting with both humans and animals. Even though they now inhabit the afterlife, these souls know that they have just as much reason to be in contact with humans now as they did when living. Indeed, these souls go into the physical lifetime fully aware that their years spent on earth are just one half of the equation. Some would say the majority of their life's purpose was to be accomplished after they die!

You need never worry or concern yourself about your death. Spirit guides say, "We know this is much easier said by us than done by you. However, it is true." At the perfect time, you will join the outward flow of life just as you joined the inward flow when you were conceived. Your existence would be much more satisfying if you allowed yourself to expand fully into the perfect scope of life you and your soul designed prior to coming in. You can trust the plan.

Do not worry about how much time you have left, or whether there will be enough time. The truth about time is that its linear nature is just packaging. A master artist uses time much more expertly than that by expanding each moment into timelessness with his or her attention. This is an enormous trade secret! Time is like taffy: it can be stretched, folded, and manipulated by your own hand using attention and focus. If you can master this viewpoint and practice it daily, by the time you die you will feel as though you have lived forever by drawing all the goodness out of each and every moment.

Chapter Three

Looking back on the summer following second grade, I wish I could have been there to hold my childhood self and reassure her: *everything is going to be okay, I promise. It's not your fault. You will get through this and life will be good again.* Eventually, I would be able to fulfill that wish through a shamanic healing ceremony called a soul retrieval. This would allow that grieving and frightened little girl to come home at last, to live happily and peacefully within the space of my now grown-up heart. At the time, however, my spiritual homecoming was still decades away.

It was a sunny summer morning in June and I woke up to the sound of my dad yelling angrily. *Happy Father's Day,* I thought, ironically. *No celebrating today, that's for sure.*

Sighing, I sat up in bed. I could hear my mom raising her voice in retaliation. Unfortunately, this kind of thing was becoming more and more common in our household. My parents' marriage had begun teetering like a seesaw. There was something different about this particular morning, though, because their voices sounded especially intense. I felt a growing sense of alarm, and sharp prickles of anxiety began scurrying up the skin on my arms and neck. This wasn't just an argument, this was a fight, and it was accelerating dangerously.

My father lashed out physically—violently—crossing an irrevocable line that day that broke our family apart. Later, when the fallout settled and the aftermath took shape, he would understand, with unbearable regret, that whenever one projects their pain onto others, there is an inevitable kickback. And unless a foundation of self-awareness and self-love has been applied to cushion this recoiling blow, it will take you down.

During my parents' subsequent separation and divorce, life became chaotic and confusing. I struggled to find solid ground in the middle of what felt like an earthquake. Desperately, I tried to hold onto as many happy memories as my heart could carry. Within a few months, both my parents were in new partnerships, and within a year both were remarried and immersed in building new lives with new partners who had their own children. I couldn't keep up; I needed more time to integrate the destruction of our family before I could even begin to imagine welcoming in a new family of strangers.

ಬಂ ೞ

In 11th century Tibet, the Indian (Bengali) Buddhist Master Atiśa wrote in *Lamp for the Path to Enlightenment* that we must train the mind to transform adversity into enlightenment. Life is not shy when it comes to doling out plenty of opportunities to test this teaching. Apparently, our family signed up for the crash course that year.

ಬಂ ೞ

"Your dad is dead."

My mother's eyes looked past me as she moved the phone receiver away from her ear, burying it in that little dip between neck and collarbone, while she said these words. Then she began sliding down the wall and would have crumpled to the kitchen floor if my stepfather's secretary, Jan—who had stopped by earlier—hadn't caught her just in time. They both sagged heavily against the wall and my mother started to sob.

In my memory, it seemed as though time stopped dead in its tracks on that cold and gray November afternoon. And not just time; everything else too. I suddenly felt as though I was standing inside a still shot of this scene, with my mother's words, "your dad is dead," ricocheting inside my head. The information wouldn't land anywhere. I heard the words, but they held no meaning. It was as if my brain was trying to figure out which address to convey this message to, and there was none. Undeliverable.

My mother and I drove together to my sister's junior high school, as she would not have heard the news yet. It occurred to me that she still existed in the world where our father was alive. I stayed in the car while my mother entered the building. My mind immediately began organizing reality into two distinct compartments: the world where my dad lived, and the world where my dad was dead. I now sat in the stands as an observer, casually noticing my focus shift back and forth like a tennis ball (this state persisted for several weeks and, as an adult, I would learn it was a type of psychological shock known as acute stress disorder). Many long minutes passed as I waited. Finally, along the line of doorways at the school's entrance, one door opened. My mother struggled to emerge as she attempted to hold my sister upright. Her legs weren't working right and they kept collapsing like a newborn colt. With arms around each other, they staggered down the path. And I watched my sister make her journey into the world where our father was dead.

I have forgotten the precise moment I finally learned how my dad died. I imagine, in the same way a medically induced coma might be necessary in cases of catastrophic injury, the memory of learning that he chose suicide over remaining here with us is sometimes still too much to consciously bear. In life, he had been unable to transform his pain and the darkness swallowed him. In death, I would come to understand, he woke up and everything was filled with light.

⁂

I am astounded and inspired by the amount of pain humans can endure and survive. Life on this planet can play very rough sometimes, leaving us grasping onto any tendril of hope we can find while dangling over the cliff's edge. Read any meaningful biography and you will find at least one story within that brings you to your knees and breaks your heart.

When I consider the miracle of human resilience, I think of Dr. Viktor Frankl. He was an Austrian neurologist and psychiatrist who was deported to Nazi-occupied Czechoslovakia to live in a Jewish ghetto for two years, along with his wife, parents, and siblings. Just prior to the liberation by the Americans in 1945, his entire family was sent to the death camps. Only Viktor and his sister survived.

Frankl wrote a well-known book about his experience called *Man's Search for Meaning*. He proposed that, despite living in the most depraved conditions imaginable, a human being's sense of significance and life purpose can persevere through conscious choice. This means that even though you may have no control over circumstances, you are always in control of what you think and how you react. During his internment, he began to identify specific qualities that seemed to enable some in the camps to maintain a will to live while others lost theirs. This eventually led to his introduction of a new type of psychoanalysis he called *logotherapy*, which offered an unconventional cure for psychospiritual wounds. Harold S. Kushner, rabbi laureate and author, wrote in the foreword to *Man's Search for Meaning*: "The greatest task for anyone is to find meaning in his or her life. Frankl saw three possible sources for meaning: in work (doing something significant), in love (caring for another person), and in courage during difficult times. Suffering in and of itself is meaningless; we give our suffering meaning by the way in which we respond to it."

Critics have been harsh, however, offering evidence to suggest Frankl made false claims about his time in Auschwitz and Dachau. Some of his peers believed his therapeutic approach reflected an inflated sense of authority and an exaggerated simplicity regarding treatment of profound mental and emotional trauma. Many would agree, however, that he can be credited with knowing far more about human suffering and survival than most. His findings and methods have helped thousands of patients, students, and practitioners over many generations since World War II. Perhaps his parents were prescient of their son's life purpose and his will to conquer devastating odds when they named him Viktor.

We are stronger than we know. My father's death (along with the chaotic events leading up to that day and the profound healing that was required long after) forged an indestructible inner strength that has contributed to every achievement and triumph I have experienced since.

What I had not yet learned about strength, however, is that you must be mindful to temper it with softness now and then, otherwise it grows into a suit of armor. And while suits of armor are vital on a battlefield, they can make it difficult for anyone to hug you once the fighting is over.

Chapter Four

G*od, I hate it here,* I thought to myself.

It was the first day of sixth grade and I was in a brand-new town. The past three years had been a whirlpool of unsettling change and my feelings of sadness had begun to harden into resentment. That summer, my mother and stepfather packed all of us—my sister, two new stepbrothers, both cats, and me—into a three-car caravan and moved us four hundred (felt like a million) miles away. Behind me was everything I had known and everyone I loved: grandmothers, aunts, uncles, cousins, and childhood friends. My sister is nearly five years older than me, and at that point in our lives there might as well have been twenty-five years between us. I was eleven, she was sixteen. As adults, we would become each other's champion and confidante, but back then we were worlds apart. The traumatic events early in our lives had not brought us closer together. Rather, they had landed us on separate shores of survival with an ocean of pain and sorrow in between.

My sense of disconnection that autumn was deep and persistent. I was aware I had built a moat around myself; I just didn't know how to break it down and remain strong on the inside. So, there I sat, back slumped against the hard brick wall of the school's main entryway; the very last kid waiting to leave for the day. *Where is the stupid bus?* I rolled my eyes in irritation.

Without warning—like a lightning bolt one becomes aware of the split second after it strikes—a blur of a boy flew past me, his arms raised and ready to bulldoze the front doors of the school wide open. He disappeared into the bright afternoon sunshine. I felt a jolt all the way to the deepest cells in my bones. There was no rational explanation for this. I didn't know him, and I hadn't seen him clearly at all. I wouldn't have been able to come close to picking him out of a lineup. I was aware he had a lot of dark hair. Obviously, he was a fast runner, and strong; it seemed as though those heavy school doors almost tore off their hinges.

That's all I knew. Yet it wasn't all I knew. In that blinkof-an-eye flurry, a sense of knowing him and knowing everything about him hit me like a cyclone. I couldn't tell you his name, but I would swear to you, in that instant, I had known him since the beginning of time. And not only that, but I also knew, somehow, that he was very dear to me. The state of his heart and happiness was important to me.

What? I shook my head. *Was I dreaming? What just happened?* I felt disoriented and jittery, like waking up on a spinning merry-go-round. Abruptly, the ride stopped and there I was again, waiting for my bus in the late afternoon silence. I knew I hadn't hallucinated all of this. I knew it meant something profound. I knew that moment activated something deep inside and I would never be the same again. Who was this boy and how would I find him again? Light began to show through chinks in my suit of armor.

It turned out he was a new kid starting sixth grade too, assigned to the classroom next to mine. And once he became aware of me too, our decades-long story began. It read like a treasure map winding through territories of friendship, love, parting, and reunion. As we grew, I began to sense that perhaps we were *resuming* an age-old epic tale of two creative souls playing with changes of scenery, dialogue, and character over lifetimes.

In the end, though, this chapter would wind down as time, distance, and circumstances led us on different life paths. The profound soul connection remained, however, as it does when love is real. And I will always remember that singular, powerful moment when he ran past me because it broke the spell of sadness and brought me back to life. Even then, at eleven years old, I pondered how I could feel so deeply impacted, so quickly, by someone I had never seen before.

The isolating armor I had built for support and protection fell away over the next couple of years as I encountered important new people who lovingly, and with much laughter, filled the holes in my heart that were left by those who had said goodbye. These new friends would become my beloved tribe of kindred spirits who are, to this very day, among the most important people in my life.

8003

We are here to relate. We do that by first believing we are singular. Like a lone castaway wandering our island, we feel deserted—until we see another castaway across the distance, inhabiting their own island. We are magnetically drawn to them as they are to us. That is when the Universe, sitting on the sidelines in its director's chair, yells, "action!" The drama plays out and a new story is created.

Soul families, soul tribes, soul mates: these are our eternal friends and relations. We have known them longer than time. Some join the party for a lifetime and incarnate with us. Some choose to watch from the bleachers, cheering us on. They laugh with love at our missteps, and cry with us when our hearts break. Then, when it is time and the festivities wind down for that particular incarnation, we joyously reunite. The returning partiers may need to take it a little slow at first, though. A lifetime spent on planet Earth can leave a soul with a bit of a vibrational hangover. Squinting with our soul eyes, wincing at the brightness, we implore our soul friends to speak a little more softly. "Tell me again, and speak nice and slow," we say. "What just happened? I was where, exactly?"

Part II

The Initiation

৪৩ ৫৪

Chapter Five

I cut my psychic teeth on the written work of Jane Roberts. Starting in the 1960s and spanning over twenty-five years, she trance-channeled an energy personality calling itself Seth while her husband, Rob, took shorthand dictation with pen and paper. The result is an extensive and genius collection of material having to do with the Universal and multidimensional nature of reality. I recommend their books to any dedicated student of metaphysics and spirituality.

It was 1986 and I was twenty-one, newly married, and excited about our recent move to Seattle. Eager to start a career, I loved my new job as a fashion merchandising assistant for a popular and trendy clothing manufacturer headquartered in the center of the bustling downtown retail core. Our division was called "Missy & Junior Wovens" and this included design and development of non-knit apparel such as jeans, blouses, and jackets. Every day, boxes filled with style samples arrived from factories in Hong Kong and Macau, resulting in stacks of acid-washed denim, neon-colored cotton cloth, and shoulder pads as far as the eye could see. We carried full-size cans of Aqua Net in our handbags and wore stirrup pants with our pumps. This was pre-grunge, pre-Nirvana—just before the alternative rock tidal wave overtook Seattle—and I was in heaven.

The fashion of the 80s appealed to me because of its graphic design elements. This appreciation would eventually lead to art school and a twelve-year career as a commercial graphic designer and advertising art director. On this particular day, however, I was in my usual workday groove, riding the elevator from our top floor office to the traffic below where I would dash across the street to pick up lunch at my favorite department store, Frederick & Nelson. For any longtime Seattleites who may be reading, I am talking about their flagship location at Fifth and Pine, home of the famous Frango candy and the best Caesar salad in town. During this time, they also had a marvelous book section in the basement level, a precursor to the giant Barnes & Noble that would move in one block away following the department store's final death rattle in 1992.

I was shopping for a good novel that I could sink my

teeth into while eating my salad and was drifting from the uninteresting new releases display into the romance section. I hadn't been a romance novel reader since my junior high school days.

I was just about to give up on the whole book-buying venture for the day and head to the escalator—I needed to get back soon and finish filling out new purchase orders for the telex operator—when I felt a sharp pain squarely on top of my head. Shocked, tears quickly welled in my eyes and my sight grew shimmery. A light fluttering sensation ran down my left leg, stopping at my foot. I looked down through the blur of pain-induced tears and saw a purple-colored paperback lying on its side, propped against my ankle.

I bent over, picked it up, and immediately winced, though not from pain. The book's cover image was disturbing. It was a photograph of a woman's face bent unnaturally sideways, her mouth open and teeth bared. Her large, dark eyes almost bulged and they seemed to look directly into mine. I nearly threw the book. It felt electric and somehow alive. I was no stranger to horror writing; by this time I had read my fair share of Stephen King. This book felt different though, and without knowing anything about it, I sensed it was important. Its title was *Seth Speaks* and the author was Jane Roberts.

Before I knew it, I was signing my name on the charge card slip and walking out into the sunshine with the book in a signature white and forest-green Frederick & Nelson shopping bag. I felt vaguely confused and disappointed. Why had I purchased this weird-looking book? I didn't even know what it was about, and I wasn't remotely motivated to find out. This kind of heedless purchase was not typical for me, particularly when it came to books. I had always been an avid reader and appreciator of books, having come from a family of serious readers who are curious and love to learn. And yet, here I stood, lunchtime winding down, holding a book I was certain I would never read.

And I didn't—that is, not until a year or so later, when I was under doctor's orders to rest in bed for a couple of days. A few weeks earlier, my husband and I had been stunned and excited to learn that I was pregnant. We were just beginning to adjust to the idea that we would soon be a family of three when I experienced a miscarriage.

I would physically recover quickly, as my body was strong and healthy. Healing the raw emotions battering our tender hearts would take longer, requiring patience and understanding. My mind felt weary and I looked for a distraction. Carefully I sat up as my body was still in some pain and reached to open the nightstand cabinet. I hoped there would be something interesting within, a book or magazine, perhaps. I stretched a little farther and felt the corner of a paperback book. Pulling it back with me into the bed, I saw that long-forgotten purple cover. Of all the books

I could have stashed in there, it had to be *Seth Speaks*. *Well,* I thought, *I might as well have a look.*

I was hooked from the very first page of the introduction. Metaphysical, spiritual, and philosophical concepts about life, death, and creation unfolded page after page. My mind, now sharp, exploded with incredulous recognition. It was as if this book was reflecting to me the thoughts and beliefs I had naturally (and secretly) held my entire life, which I had mostly buried in the years following my father's death. A sense of relief and remembrance flooded my entire being. *I'm not the only one who sees the world this way,* I thought excitedly. *I am not alone.*

From that moment on, my curiosity was unquenchable. I read every Jane Roberts book I could find and began to regard Seth, Jane, and her husband, Rob, as my teachers. Over time, I would meet and study with others who shared the same passion, curiosity, and dedication. They became soul sisters and brothers and we supported, encouraged, and challenged each other on a path of discovery which would ultimately lead me to my life's work.

ॐ ☙ ❧

Our spiritual teachers and mentors come to us in a variety of ways. Whether we receive a (literal) smack on the head or we are inexplicably drawn to a lecturer who blows our mind wide open, we must first be ready, otherwise the new information will be unable to land in our current understanding. Sometimes we know when we're ready for this and sometimes we do not (and, in that case, the readiness lies within our subconscious awareness). If you look at it from an energetic perspective, it is easy to see how perfectly this works: the teacher desires to share wisdom and experience which they have been given, and the student wishes to receive new information in order to reach a greater level of understanding. This is a perpetual process which provides the necessary locomotion our Universe uses to expand, and it has been operating this way since the beginning.

Never worry about your level of comprehension or proficiency; whether beginner or master, there will always be more to learn and there will always be a source from which you may generously take. And when it is time for you to be the teacher, never worry that your contributions (lessons, books, or examples) are redundant or inconsequential. There will always be those who need to receive exactly what you are offering, in precisely the way you have prepared it. And, really, we are all teachers for one another, and we are all eternal students.

Chapter Six

The first thing I noticed after being shot in the neck was that I could no longer raise my right arm. *Curious,* I thought, as I looked down at my now useless limb. The only pain I felt was the breaking of my heart as it dawned on me that I was about to die.

The scene unfolded in reverse and the backstory revealed itself: a dark-haired woman dressed in a ruby-colored velvet coat moved quickly through the cold, damp darkness. Her long, billowing skirts whipped in waves around the scissoring motion of her legs. She was running away in the middle of the night, headed toward the waterfront. She held a bundle of blankets close to her chest, a newborn infant swaddled tightly against the chill night air. "My daughter," she said out loud into the deserted night.

The shadowy outline of an enormous sailing ship took shape in the dark distance ahead. She quickened her pace, nearly sprinting headlong toward it. She needed to board that ship and find the captain immediately. There were no other options left now. This was her only—and final—chance. She had to find him, for she loved him deeply; he was the father of the child she held in her arms.

Abruptly, the tableau shattered into a million fragments, sending my awareness spinning into the void along with them. My brain ached as it attempted to readjust and my stomach lurched against a wall of nausea. All at once, there was a mighty shift and, like a roller coaster on its track, my point of view was redirected onto an entirely new scene.

I was standing in an enclosed room, dim candlelight cast shifting shadows across the heavy wood-planking walls and low ceiling of the captain's private quarters. Where was the baby? Panicked, with my back against the farthest wall, my eyes swept the room. Straight ahead was a door. I turned my head to the left to see my daughter safely tucked into a basket. She was awake, and her face serene as her body moved gently under the wrappings. Even though we appeared to have reached our destination safely, my instincts were screaming that we were in grave danger. Fear coursed through my nervous system like wildfire, its intensity making me physically sick. Something very bad was about to happen.

The heavy door crashed open, propelling a blast of air that flattened every candle flame in the room. A man barreled through the threshold, raising a pistol directly at my face. This man, I instantly and intuitively knew, was not the captain. This man was my husband. His red face was full of rage, contorted with the effort of holding the heavy flintlock upright and steady. Without warning or explanation, he fired the gun. My ears began to ring as time seemed suddenly to be moving through heavy syrup. The bullet emerged from the muzzle and sent rings of shock waves rippling through the air, like water in a pond.

Astonished, I watched the bullet move in slow motion, straight toward my face. Heart catching in my throat, my body accelerated into survival mode. Then I saw that the bullet began to veer ever so slightly. I paused, hopeful, and rapidly reassessed the situation. Maybe it would miss its target. The bullet ruffled the air a hair's breadth from my jaw and plunged into my neck. Pain exploded like a bomb in my head and I jolted as I sat on the couch, safe in the here and now. My eyes watered as I gazed out over the city from my sixth-floor condominium.

Years before I became a practitioner, I studied many books on trance channeling. These books introduced me to the concept of the eternal nature of the soul from a metaphysical standpoint. I concluded that if the soul is indeed eternal, then the idea of reincarnation is not only fascinating and exciting, but also plausible and practical. Inspired by channeling methods, I began exploring a practice called automatic writing. This type of creative writing is considered a form of channeling if the intention is to receive information from beings in spiritual or multidimensional realms.

It was during one of these sessions where, spontaneously, I began transcribing a letter in a voice and style not my own. The words came quickly and passionately, and the cursive writing was large and embellished, completely unlike my usual penmanship. As my pen moved faster and faster, a scene unfolded, introducing me to the dark-haired woman.

The automatic writing story concluded as she realized she was dying. An overwhelming wave of grief engulfed her, and she knew she was leaving behind her newborn baby and her beloved captain. Mentally, she resolved to watch over them in the after-death state to make sure they stayed safe. With relief, she began to intuitively understand that they would escape without harm. They would travel to a new place and make a peaceful and prosperous life there. The captain would lovingly raise their daughter, forging an inseparable bond with her. Comforted by certainty, she felt free to let go and make her transition to the other side. Before she did, an astonishing thing occurred; she turned her attention directly to me as I sat immersed in the automatic writing state. She spoke to me directly through the words I wrote onto the page in front of me:

Dear Meaghan,

Trust this process. We are connected, you and I. Indeed, we are the same—we spring from the same source. The souls in this story are the very same souls you know within your own family. The tale continues and you have much to learn from one another. We are given many opportunities to choose forgiveness and love.

Ever Your Friend,

Dominique

Bath, 1746

The entire incredible session had lasted only a few minutes, although it felt like lifetimes had passed. Had I really communicated with a woman named Dominique who lived and died 250 years earlier in Bath, England? And was I somehow that woman? And was she, me? My mind swam trying to fit this extraordinary story into a logical box. However, my heart felt sure and at peace with the knowledge.

In the back of mind, I recalled my lifelong sensitivity about the right side of my neck. To this day, whenever I feel anxious or afraid, my neck tingles and twitches and I raise my right shoulder in a protective gesture. I feel physically uncomfortable if someone merely glances at that side of my neck.

ঞ ৩

I developed an insatiable curiosity about past lives after this experience and began to read every book I could get my hands on that might help me to understand this phenomenon better. This ultimately led me to a book called *Many Lives, Many Masters* by Brian L. Weiss, MD. Dr. Weiss graduated from Yale Medical School and is Chairman Emeritus of Psychiatry at the Mount Sinai Medical Center in Miami, Florida. He began using past life regression therapy in private practice in the 1980s and has since treated thousands of patients. After writing numerous books on the topic, Dr. Weiss began lecturing and teaching around the world.

In early 2000, I had the pleasure and honor of meeting Dr. Weiss in person. He was speaking at the Seattle Opera house, which was a short walk from my Queen Anne neighborhood home. By then, I had become a great admirer of his work, having read all the books he had written. The moment I heard he was coming to town, I bought my ticket and signed up to attend a wine reception with him following his lecture. The evening of the event, I arrived at the auditorium an hour early and was the first person there. I immediately found a seat in the very first row, front and center—I did not want to miss a single thing!

When he finally walked onstage, an energy of serenity,

kindness, and care was immediately palpable. It was like a wave washing over the entire audience and we all fell silent in its wake. His face broke into an enormous smile and he softly spoke into the microphone, "Hello everyone, I'm very happy to be here with you this evening." He went on to talk about the many ways he had come to use and appreciate the healing benefits of past life regression work.

He told us it was possible to cure debilitating trauma, phobias, and physical illnesses with this modality. These were bold and inspiring claims, although his body of work along with the case histories had already proven his statements to be true. He also shared with us the importance of exploring what happens after death and before the next birth (a period often referred to as "life in between lifetimes"). Hundreds of patient hypnotherapy sessions showed him that this was an important time of review, integration, and planning for the soul. I sat in my seat with rapt attention, hanging on every word and writing notes at full speed.

Afterward, a large group of us met in a private room adjacent to the auditorium where Dr. Weiss would be joining us in an informal social setting. I nervously approached the open bar and asked for a glass of wine, thankful to have something to calm my excitement about meeting one of my heroes in person.

The room began to buzz as I watched Dr. Weiss walk through the door. Immediately, he became mobbed by a dozen people. I felt sorry for him; I wouldn't want so many people swarming around me like that, even though they were doing it in a kindly manner. He didn't look perturbed in the least though, and that same peaceful, open energy he exuded on the stage in the auditorium was present here too. *Amazing,* I thought, *he manages his personal space so skillfully and with such love.* I was impressed.

I put aside my uneasiness as an even larger group advanced toward him and merged into the flow in order to make my way closer. I continued to sip my wine and smile at those around me who were also hoping for a chance to meet the renowned and beloved doctor. Finally, my turn was next. I could feel my heart racing and my hands beginning to shake. No doubt about it, I was starstruck. Smiling widely, I extended my hand to shake his and exclaimed, "It is such an honor to meet you, Dr Weiss!" To my horror, I realized that I was simultaneously shaking his hand like a cracking whip while moving my other hand up and down in unison. I sprayed wine all over myself and the white sweater I was wearing.

Dr. Weiss calmly looked into my eyes and with a small, amused smile on his face said, "Aren't you glad you went with the white wine tonight?" The spell was broken as I laughed out loud. Taking a deep breath, I could feel myself come back into my body and become grounded. I thanked him, told him my name, and asked him if I could get his opinion about something. "Of course," he said.

I shared with him that I would one day like to do the type of work he does, but I didn't want to spend years in school to become qualified. Did he think it was important to go through all of that and obtain the degrees, credentials, and certifications?

He said he believed it was possible to do this work well without jumping through traditional hoops; however, my access would be limited. In other words, the world at large is still invested in, is comforted by, and trusts conventional accomplishments. Becoming professionally trained would give me keys to doors I would not otherwise be able to walk through. I felt the truth and wisdom of his advice and thanked him. He smiled warmly and turned his attention to the next person who was eagerly awaiting their turn.

It was cold, dark, and rainy as I walked beneath the Space Needle, heading home after the event. I was deep in thought, reviewing all that had transpired that evening. My heart felt full of gratitude and emotion. I looked up to see Dr. Weiss, alone, walking briskly toward a car idling by the curb. I opened my mouth to shout good night and immediately decided not to disturb him. He turned then and looked at me, smiling. He mouthed a silent good night, waved, and disappeared into the waiting car.

ಬಾ ಅ

Past life regression work is fascinating on so many levels. Whether you have a belief in reincarnation or not, the process opens up an entirely new world full of characters, places, and events that unfold to reveal mythic heroic tales of every sort. Every culture passes down its wisdom through some form of storytelling. These healing, evolutionary dramas reflect the creative process your own soul uses to grow.

You have lived many, many times. And you will likely live many, many more. Like a stone skipping on a still lake, you touch down upon the fabric of corporeal life in an ever-increasing outward spiral of experience. To the soul, existence is experienced multidimensionally and, like this book you are now reading, can be organized by sections and chapters. These may be arranged in any sequence, in any direction, and in any form. Being a human on planet Earth is merely one form of an infinite amount of forms. I say "infinite" because every time a soul takes on a form to express, it is then inspired by that experience to activate other forms that are new. Therefore, this process is automatically exponential—not only for you but for other souls too.

Reincarnation could be considered a legacy you hand down to yourself. It is a multidimensional gift of greater perspective. Each of us become Universal diplomats born with the unique ability to experience all roles: the lover, the outlaw, the ruler, the slave, the warrior, the mother, the brother, and anything else you and the Great Mystery can conjure.

Chapter Seven

"I want you to name your greatest fear."

My teacher announced this to the circle of students gathered in the main room of a remote cabin located deep in the Pacific Northwest rainforest. It was my first year of formal shamanic training. We were gathered for a weekend intensive retreat, the first of many initiatory experiences I would experience over the next several years.

What if I am crazy? I thought. There it was. Finally, the acknowledgement of my greatest fear.

It was time to ask this question, in all seriousness. And it was time to know the answer. Could it be true that all this psychic and spiritual stuff I had been drawn to my entire life was nothing more than a giant delusion? It was a possibility I had to consider, and this was the perfect time and place to find out.

The road leading to this day had begun when my husband and I decided to divorce after fifteen years of marriage. Our beautiful baby daughter had been born five years earlier and her arrival burst my heart wide open. I had no idea it was possible to experience love at such a deep and profound level. Waking up every morning to her smiling face was an indescribable joy and every minute of every day became a blessing.

The light of her arrival also revealed the long-standing cracks in our marriage. I had to accept that her father and I were not happy together. He and I both knew it, and neither of us wanted that for ourselves, or each other. Even though it meant raising our daughter separately, I knew she would benefit from growing up with a mother who was living honestly, healthfully, and powerfully. I vowed to do all that I could to love, nurture, and provide so that she might know her true strength and love herself and others with a full and open heart.

Part of this vow included nurturing and healing myself as much as possible, on every level: emotionally, mentally, physically, and spiritually. My wish was to become the mother she most needed me to be, and at the same time become the woman I most needed to be for myself. I jumped into the deep end because . . . why not? I had just pulled down the entire framework of my life; there was no reason not to get in there and start over from the ground up.

My efforts included more physical activity, and my body craved anything that pushed it beyond the limit of endurance. At the time, I was a graphic designer and my biggest client was located near the top of a fifty-story high-rise building. During lunch breaks, I would sprint up and down the vast stairwell that coiled from the ground like a gigantic strand of DNA. I couldn't get enough. My body was finally able to fully open, pulling in the life-giving oxygen needed to build the strength and power it had been craving for years.

Equally as important was the emotional and mental work I was doing. I devoured books on meditation, spirituality, self-help, and metaphysics. I started crafting a deeply personal and committed spiritual practice, thanks to the authors who became my beloved teachers. I also began working with a counselor and massage therapist who cooperated on each other's cases. It was a brilliant setup and one I hadn't seen before or since. For every one or two private sessions I had with the counselor, the three of us would then meet up at the massage therapist's office. While the counselor and I talked, the massage therapist targeted locations in my body that were triggered by the emotions I was feeling and the memories I was unearthing. This helped my body release my past trauma the moment I remembered it. It was swift, strong, and effective work that allowed me to break through old stories that had been holding me back since childhood.

It was during one of these sessions that the massage therapist mentioned she was working with a shamanic practitioner to heal her own issues. A shamanic practitioner? I had never heard the term before and had no idea what, or who, that was. She explained that shamanism was an ancient healing practice that incorporated earth medicine and indigenous ceremonial practices. I listened intently; however, I still had no clue what she was talking about. What is *earth* medicine? Earth medicine, she went on, works with the natural world to bring about healing by using plants, animals, stones, the elements, and seasonal forces.

As she spoke, something inside me began to shift. I couldn't tell if it was a longing I felt, or an old memory finally surfacing. Suddenly, a clear and intense understanding settled in my core. I asked her for the name of the shamanic practitioner. Instinctively, I understood that until this point, I had never fully recognized or connected with the planet, with Mother Earth. I had spent most my life either living in my head or completely disconnected from my body. Now, I needed to be *here*.

One year later, after meeting and working with the shamanic practitioner, I was participating in her healing circle and training to become certified in shamanic energy medicine practices. At that time, I wasn't planning on becoming a practitioner; I was learning and sharing this experience with the other students as a way to continue my personal healing journey. I wanted to absorb as much as possible about this fascinating community that the Universe had invited me into. I had never felt so alive, so a part of the intelligence of our planet and all her beings. This healing path was the road leading me to my true home.

The training and teachings were arduous. Mother Earth and her lessons were direct and practical. Like any good mom, she did not mess around. Her message to me was loving, yet firm: show up, get well, love more, and move on with your purpose. This medicine was not esoteric or subtle. Although it was full of wisdom and the supernatural, it was well-grounded and functional. It dared me to become clear, present, and truthful. This was not a conceptual approach to living. This was as real as it got—and I loved it. I was growing braver, bolder, and stronger every day.

"I want you to name your greatest fear," my teacher repeated firmly. Her gaze moved slowly around the circle, focusing intently on each one of us with bright, clear blue eyes that tracked everything and missed nothing.

We were about to invite our greatest fear to come up right into our faces so that we could take a good, long look. The purpose of this exercise was to acknowledge and understand what terrorized and bedeviled us. It was an opportunity to become masterful, a way to grow ability and authority. And the best way to master a thing is to know a thing, intimately.

My biggest fear, I already knew, was that my lifelong (and now rapidly growing) psychic abilities were really nothing more than expressions of insanity. As incomprehensible as it sounded, even after a lifetime of talking with Spirit, a part of me still wondered if I was just crazy. As time went on and I met and worked with other psychics, I learned that this is a common fear. Even for those of us who grew up supported in our supernatural beliefs, it can be difficult to accept our experiences in a culture that persecutes those who dare to live their lives out loud.

I was finally ready to face this fear, this integral and deep part of my identity. Naming your greatest fear is easy if you're being razor-sharp honest with yourself. To do this, you must hunker down into the spiritual mud. You can't name fears correctly from your intellect, no; fear lives in the belly, and it shoots arrows of icy fear up into the heart. This is primordial terrain and it won't tolerate being ordered or organized. It doesn't recognize common sense, and its instinct to survive is strong, stronger than your will and your logic. It knows every backdoor and crack to slither through.

In order to access this place, we were to be guided on a spiritual, mystical meditation facilitated by our teacher. She called this a shamanic journey. It would be a long one and we would need all that time because we were not only naming our greatest fear, we had to sit with it. We couldn't run, ignore, or deny it any longer. We were to sit with it long enough to listen and fully understand it. So long, in fact, that we would finally see it for what it really is, and it would no longer be a fear, but a healing story telling us something valuable.

The most terrifying aspect of your greatest fear is learning that it may actually be true—which is why most of us avoid examining our fears. We somehow find it more tolerable to run away from, or even be run by, our fears. We will run from some fears for decades and be consumed or tortured by the awareness of it in our peripheral mind vision. Its presence keeps us ever vigilant, never able to fully relax into anything in our lives. Why do we not stop, take a breath, sit down, and invite our fear to the table? Why do we not let it say its piece? Because, again, we may no longer be able to deny that our biggest fear is, indeed, true. And if it is true, then it might mean we are, indeed, terrible. Or irreparably flawed. Or sinful. Or crazy.

What if we *are*? What if one, or all, of these things are true? What then? Does it mean that all is lost? We seem unable to hold enough self-love to accept the worst of who we are. Things we might forgive or overlook in others become unforgivable when applied to ourselves. Who or what dictates what the worst is, anyway? One person's "dreadful!" is another person's "who cares?"

Self-love. If our ability to love ourselves is greater than our fears, we will find footing to stay and not run away. We will commit to ourselves instead of abandoning ourselves. We will say, "I am here, I am present, and I am going nowhere, no matter what." That is self-love. That is where we find the intelligence and the strength to not only name our greatest fear but lift it out of the mud and into its potential. This is the transformation. This is the miracle. This is how we love ourselves. We identify, understand, and love those parts of ourselves that we most fear.

So, I sat. And I waited. Eventually, my greatest fear began to reveal itself. Slowly, at first, and from far in the distance. It was no more than a pinprick of light shining in the vast darkness I had banished it to years ago when I realized that people might react negatively to this aspect of myself. As I focused on relaxing, opening, and observing without judgement, the light grew larger as it came closer. I sensed an intelligence within the light, an equilibrium. I became curious and mentally leaned toward it. As it approached, the ball of light grew to a size that matched my own, if not a little larger. It stopped and rested about four feet in front of me and just to my right. And so we sat for several long moments.

Finally, I decided to turn my full attention toward it, feeling just brave and curious enough to see this fear for what it truly was, even if that meant accepting my psychic abilities as nothing more than an expression of mental illness. I turned and looked. Surprisingly, I felt it turn toward me. It was patiently present and not what I expected "crazy" to feel like. Suddenly the ball of light started laughing at me.

The sound startled me at first, but soon began to scare me as it grew louder and more forceful. The laughter detonated in the darkness, sending shock waves of sound flapping around me like bats in a cave. It took all my strength and presence to remain in the meditation. *Don't run! Don't run! Don't run!* I chanted to myself over and over, until I sensed a small, deep core of calm growing in the pit of my stomach. I breathed deeply, and as I exhaled the calm began to light up my chest and extend out to my limbs and up my neck and into my head. The raucous laughter died down.

Who are you? What are you? I asked the light.

"I am your greatest fear," it replied. "And one of your greatest gifts."

Why all the crazy laughter?

"Your belief about insanity has grown over many years of intense focus. This energy became strong enough to evolve into its own identity. You expect the worst, therefore, reality has no choice but to comply. I am the reflection of your most feared outcome."

I sat silently now, open to understanding more. The light explained that cloaking my abilities with the label of "crazy" was an easy excuse. It enabled me to avoid stepping deeply into one of my biggest reasons for being in this lifetime. Unfortunately, it also kept me small and unable to express myself fully. I had become afraid of feeling unafraid. What would it mean if I didn't have to play small? What would happen if I allowed myself free reign to use all the abilities I had been gifted with in this lifetime?

Likely, embracing my abilities fully would mean those who lived in fear themselves would see my choices as threatening or scary. I would have to experience leaving these relationships behind. This should have felt bad, but instead it felt freeing. I felt lighter. How long had I been carrying this burden of believing I had to be like everyone else in order to be accepted? How long I had believed I needed the approval of others so I could survive?

I could, and would, survive on my own. Not as an island so much as a resource. Taking care of myself felt like a sacred blessing, and entirely doable. Moment by moment, I felt stronger. The light came closer and closer to me now, and I gratefully brought it into myself. This had been a vital and integral piece of my being, of who I truly was. I had spent almost my entire life up to that point treating it as an aberration, something wrong, scary, or dangerous. This fear was not a fear at all. It was mislaid creativity, ability, compassion, and strength. It was one of the most important gifts I was meant to share in this lifetime!

Wave after wave of understanding dawned on me. My

greatest fear had revealed itself to be my greatest strength and I was free at last.

ΩΩ⊗

Fear is potent, possibly one of the most potent substances for causing destruction on the planet. It makes us believe there are no solutions, and robs us of our ability to choose. This stands against everything we are about. We are creators; we sprang from the Creative Source and we are always connected to it, even when fear would have us believe otherwise.

Fear stymies our ability to carry out our primary objective: to create freely. How does this need to create mesh with life on this planet when all around us are seemingly countless reasons to stop in our tracks from fear, throw up our hands, and surrender to powerlessness? Ah, but see, there it is again. Must we surrender? Are we, indeed, powerless? Even in the face of impossible odds? We are always able to reorient ourselves from what appears in the present moment to be a fearful situation. We can always choose how we opt to see the issue.

That is the gift of free will. Free will could also be called Creative Expression. They are one and the same. This is the ultimate superpower that disarms all fear, even in the most dire and life-threatening situations. This understanding is the substance of all heroes. A hero is one who continues to pivot, continues to look from a new perspective, no matter how slight. From that fresh position, they have no option but to find a solution, a way to move forward. If we can just remember this and apply it to our own lives, each of us can be heroes.

The next time your fear comes forward, sit with it for a while. Ask it to show itself to you so that you may understand its genius. Typically, we look for the solution everywhere except the middle of our fears. Why not jump right in and see what you're missing?

Part III

The Calling

ಬಿ೦೦೦

Chapter Eight

A woman stood in the doorway and hesitated for a moment. Immediately, I saw the image of a fragrant white flower crushed under the stacked black heel of a dusty cowboy boot. My mind searched for the correct name of the blossom. Gardenia? Magnolia? The bruised and flattened petals, once delicate and graceful, had already started to yellow and would soon turn brown. These pictures, of course, were playing across my inner, psychic vision. I readjusted my focus, smiled, and welcomed the woman—who was not part of my vision, but was here, now—into the closet-sized room in the back of the metaphysical bookstore where I met clients for their readings.

This was back in the early days of my healing and intuitive practice. A fellow psychic, who had also become a friend, challenged me to go beyond the "boutique readings" (his words) that I was offering to friends from the safety and comfort of my home. He urged me to venture into the world where I might be able to help people who "really needed it" (again, his words). I took him up on the dare out of a conflicting mixture of defiance and a desire to serve. Who was he to pass judgment on how I conducted my work? *Boutique readings, indeed! What does that even mean?*

I have since wondered if he knew exactly what he was doing by throwing down the perfect gauntlet to stir up the competitive side of my nature. He had an astute psychic ability and a razor-sharp tongue to go with it, and he never sugarcoated his words. This was to become his trademark teaching style as a practitioner, and it seldom failed to motivate clients and students to rise up and push past self-imposed limitations. It certainly worked on me.

Rising from my seat in the dimly lit room, I greeted the young woman. She was in her twenties, tall and slender, fashionably dressed. Outwardly, she looked put together, with freshly styled hair, tastefully applied makeup, and coordinated accessories. However, these details migrated to the back of my awareness as her energy began to paint an entirely different picture. It filled the cramped space, and the psychic images she projected did not match the story she showed the outer world.

I offered her a seat, gesturing to the folding office chair across from the small table where I would be arranging the tarot cards. Although I no longer use divination tools (like cards, runes, I Ching coins, or a pendulum) during client sessions, at that time I did. In addition to their oracular usefulness, the cards also served as a focal point for both my client and I, offering us something to anchor our gaze upon. Early into my psychic career, however, the information I received from Spirit began channeling so quickly I would end up laying the cards down and allowing the information to flow on its own as I spoke.

The young woman sat down nervously, spine straight, leaning forward over the purse placed in her lap. I spoke with her for a minute or two, letting her know how the reading would begin and what to expect. She relaxed a little, sighed, and a small smile softened the sad tension in her face. As with every client session I have ever facilitated, I began with a prayer said aloud. This was an invitation and intention that only the good, true, and beautiful of the spirit realm were welcome to bring forward healing information. I asked, as I still do, that this work serve the highest good and greatest joy of all concerned—for this generation and the next seven generations.

Before I could finish the prayer, the cowboy boot returned, looming large in my psychic vision. It began to grow, becoming a dark shadow in the shape of a man. Right away, I could sense this woman had an extensive history of being mistreated by the men in her life. This shadow figure didn't represent one single man; it represented many men, from childhood to the present, in both her personal and professional realms. Understanding broke through my awareness like light rays through a storm cloud. The white flower I had seen earlier represented this woman sitting in front of me. Her relationships with men were crushing her spirit, and this had been happening for most, if not all, her life. As an adult, she had taken this pattern of unhealthy boundaries to an ultimate expression with her profession: she was a prostitute.

This was her job and she was very good at it. And I don't mean the sexual part; she was an empath who had become dissociated from the physical part of her job description quite a while ago. She was successful in her work because people were drawn to her abilities as a natural-born counselor and healer. Although beginning to fade, she emanated a graceful and nurturing light that drew those who needed to be seen and held.

Unfortunately, her life path up to that point had only shown her how to express and share these abilities in a way that depleted and harmed her. When she was with a man, her boundaries dissolved on every level: physical, emotional, spiritual, and mental. Like a weathervane, she shifted with every whim her client projected, constantly recalibrating and redirecting her energy. She was exhausted and coming apart at the seams. She knew it, I knew it, and we both knew that was what brought her in to have a reading that day.

I began to lay the cards down into an arrangement called a "spread." This is the framework that formed the blueprint for her story. In addition, I would also receive valuable insight directly from both my spirit guides and hers. Together, all these sources helped inform me of the words I would share with my client. In this young woman's case, the resounding message was that she needed to grow strong in her conviction to maintain healthy boundaries no matter whether the men in her life liked it or not. This would feel risky at first. She would need to stay strong and push past her fears of loss—whether loss of work, money, or popularity. Her life literally depended on it, as she was suffering from depression and physical exhaustion that had begun eroding her will to live.

She listened intently and her eyes grew bright with unshed tears. I shared with her my feeling that she wasn't nearly as concerned about losing clients as she was about the prospect of never finding a healthy love relationship in her personal life. She nodded, tears finally spilling forth, making wet tracks down her cheeks. "Yes," she said, "I want true love more than anything else."

I continued. "You're afraid to say no to destructive

relationships because you don't have faith healthy love exists, or that you are worthy of it."

"Yes," she whispered, lifting her eyes to look into mine.

That's the crazy thing about love; it often requires your trust before it offers itself to you. It's a fascinating and frustrating eternal romantic paradox. The best way to build trust is by first keeping an unwavering commitment to love *yourself* before your beloved shows up. One of the most important ways to do this is by saying no to those people and situations in your life that are not uplifting, fulfilling, and nourishing.

The first few times you do this feels like running headlong over a cliff: you just keep hoping to God the parachute opens to catch your fall. Once you realize you are not falling, that you're actually *rising* and standing up for yourself, you feel exhilarated. You finally understand this has been the magic formula all along: love yourself as you would love another.

This might sound like the opposite of what children are often taught: that you should give to others before taking for yourself. I believe that if you want to offer your beloved the best possible version of yourself, you must nourish your heart with generous servings of self-love.

This does not mean you have to be perfect, or look perfect, or smell perfect, or be perfectly happy all the time. Perfection is not the goal, because perfection doesn't exist.

It is not a thing you can do, be, or have—so let that go once and for all. When you love someone deeply, you naturally want them to have the best possible everything, including the best possible version of you. The way to do this is to become as masterful as you can in the areas of self-regard and self-care. This is how you build a beautiful home in your heart to receive and write your love story with another. This is how the Universe knows you are ready for big, true, deep, and sustainable love.

Her reading ended with a prediction gleaned by peeking at the life plan her soul had written for her before she was born. She would indeed find her true love. He was already out there waiting for her, even though they both weren't aware of it yet. Her guides told her not to worry, that they were on the job and divine timing was programming the perfect set of events that would bring them together. Upon hearing this, her body involuntarily breathed deeply and fully, as if she was taking her first breath. She exhaled, shaking a little at the rush of oxygen and energy that reanimated her being. We both smiled. I said a prayer to close the session.

It was time for her to leave and she reached for her purse to pay. The shiny quilted leather of her designer clutch was fastened along the top with a chunky gold zipper that ran from one end to the other. She grabbed the metal tab, sliding it briskly along the tape, when it abruptly stopped at the midway point. Furrowing her brows, she jiggled the stubborn zipper and then tried to force it open. No luck. It was stuck fast on something inside the purse. Wiggling her thumb and forefinger, she managed to widen the small opening enough to reach inside. I stood up from my chair and leaned over the table, trying to help. That's when I saw what the zipper had caught. The muted light in the room was just powerful enough to reveal that her purse was stuffed to the brim with cash.

The zipper had caught on a wadded-up ball of what looked like twenty-dollar bills, which were hopelessly shredding with every attempt she made to pry the zipper's metal teeth open. Finally, she ripped the ruined ball of bills free and held it in her hands like a dirty tissue. Irritated, she looked around the room for a trash can. There was one just across the hall in the bathroom, though I was not about to tell her that, since it was obvious she was contemplating throwing away the money without a second thought. She shrugged her shoulders and shoved the cash back inside her purse. After rooting around a bit, she pulled out the correct amount of intact bills and handed them to me. Stunned, all I could say was thank you. She smiled warmly, thanked me, turned around and walked out.

I would see her several more times for readings over the next couple of years. Each time she came in, she seemed to grow more and more beautiful, strong, and vibrant. One day she shared that she had met a wonderful man while she was out of town at a work event. Although she never admitted that she was a sex worker, she had divulged enough information for me to understand that her profession was no different than any other when it came to business networking.

They had met in the lobby of the hotel where the event was being hosted. He was waiting on some friends who were getting settled in their room. It turned out that he had grown up in the same small town she had. It was unbelievable that they had never met. They swapped phone numbers and had been talking nonstop ever since—and he would be coming to visit her within the month.

I smiled and listened, happy to see her animated face lit up with excitement. I knew this would be her last visit and I would never see her again—and I never did. I have thought of her over the years, and the extraordinary and challenging life she had led for one so young. She had placed herself repeatedly (and literally) in positions of transactional love with numerous men in a way that allowed her to maintain the role of observer until, one day, she was finally ready to allow true love into her heart.

⁓⁔

You might assume that most of my client sessions have to do with love, and you would be correct. Love is, after all, everything. I've heard it said that love is the opposite of fear. Does love have, or even need, an opposite? I have come to understand that the Universe does not require congruency, or logical conclusions, in the way we, as material beings, believe is necessary. There really is no "if/then" at the Creation level. The Universe is multidimensional and holographic, it has progressed way beyond that kind of simple black-and-white thinking.

We dear humans however . . . well, we sometimes treat logic like oxygen. We breath it in deeply, hoping it will sustain us and believing we will perish without it. Then we go a step farther by attempting to apply logic to our love lives—big mistake, apparently. This must be why God invented poets, pastors, psychotherapists, psychics, and other pathfinders. They are the lighthouses who help us return to the safe shores of home once we have exhausted ourselves upon the stormy sea of love.

Thanks to Plato, Aristotle, and other thinkers, seekers, and mad scientists, we generally dissect love into four classic forms: Eros (passion and sex), Philia (friendship and goodwill), Storge (familial, parent/child), and Agape (universal, altruistic). If we are in a particularly geeky love mood, we might even add these categories: Ludus (playful, uncommitted), Pragma (duty, practicality), and

Philautia (self-love).

Eros, poetically speaking, is the one form that seems to incite a unique madness in us. Sometimes we confuse this single chapter of our lives with the entire love story. We attempt to live forever within the fiery excitement of passion rather than use it as a catalyst to boost us into love's higher realms. Instead, Eros should be thought of as the romantic trailhead that will, hopefully, lead us toward the more mature and multifaceted forms of love. That's the idea, anyway.

So, why does it hurt so very, very badly sometimes?

Love hurts when we attempt to constrict it, which we do when we feel scared that it might change or run away. Our love wants to grow and expand, for that is its nature. We suffer whenever we demand that it live in one room only. Love wants to live in the entire house, free to move about from room to room, form to form; from Agape to Philautia and everywhere in between.

Spirit tells me that love is energy, or more precisely that it is The Energy. It is the first and foundational element that Creation uses to make everything. When a human being loves, they are aware of and are playing with the true essence of themselves and all others. We might say about our friend, "She loves." The Universe would say, "She *is* Love." To me, this means there are no mistakes in the game of love, not really.

Even in instances of abandonment or harm, love exists. When something very bad happens and we feel pain, love is still there. It hasn't disappeared, yet we are unable to feel it because the pain now has our full attention. Here's how this works: pain of any kind, whether physical or psychological, consumes vast amounts of our energy and attention. Perception becomes skewed by the resulting deficit, causing disastrous results for everyone involved. Clear thinking flies out the window as we become overextended and overwrought. Whether your role is perpetrator or victim, it is the same process.

Think about any time you have stubbed your toe and a beloved rushed over to assist. Very likely, you felt instant irritation and impatiently waved them off, saying, "Just give me a minute!" It is so easy to lash out when we are in pain. Now multiply this simplistic example by ten, or one hundred, or more, and it is easy to imagine the power our woundedness possesses to harm others. Of course, this in no way excuses or justifies harmful choices or actions. Mistreatment should never be tolerated for any reason. What is helpful to realize, I believe, is that the illusion of lovelessness is just that: an illusion. This understanding offers extraordinary opportunities for healing and growth—and, in time, perhaps forgiveness. Whether we live happily ever after together, or intentionally apart, Love is there.

Chapter Nine

"Uh, hi." His voice was low and unsure, making it difficult to hear through the speaker on my cell phone.

"Hello," I replied.

"Gosh, I didn't think you would actually pick up. Um, I was just wondering. Do you talk to people who are . . . who have . . ." His voice trailed off.

I responded, "Yes, I do communicate with those who have passed on. Are you calling to find out about having a reading?"

"Um, well. Would you be able to talk to my dad? He died and my grandma wants to know what he wants us to do with his motorcycle."

What a great question, I thought. It was simple, straight-forward, practical, and real. I could imagine wanting to ask the Universe a question like this and then stopping myself, assuming it too mundane for the Universe's consideration. But, is it really mundane? Aren't our most personal and pressing questions the most interesting ones we have?

I don't think anything we want to ask in a session is mundane, silly, inconsequential, or a waste of time. We tend to think we want or need to know only about the really big things, like: why did he have to die? Is he ok? Does he know we love him? Of course, these are important, too. However, it is also true we may have smaller questions to ask that sound commonplace on the surface, yet to our family and friends they mean the world.

Spirit tells me all questions are important—big and small—because our words are vehicles for something more meaningful than the language we use to form the question. Our words convey emotional intensity, and these are the energy signals Spirit uses to determine what we really want to know. Communication as we learned it in school—expressing our thoughtforms using sentences, correct grammar, and other compositional skills—is a simple model. If it weren't for our inherent telepathic abilities, words would fall short as a clear method of communication (as they sometimes still do, despite telepathy). Words are the packaging that hold multifaceted meaning; the words themselves are not the meaning. When you communicate with Spirit, you do so by choice (free will), thus extending a formal invitation to the Universe. This is why your words are so important—they act like instruments. However, it is your intention within each word which actually communicates the true message.

It has now been several years since that young man courageously reached out to me on behalf of his grandmother, and I have remembered that snippet of phone conversation ever since. In the end, the family booked a reading with me and the deceased father came through to communicate. He spoke to me psychically (clairaudience) to say that he wanted his cherished motorcycle to go to his teenage nephew. That made perfect sense to the family, since this nephew was the only one who had been keeping the bike cleaned and polished since the death occurred. I later heard the nephew was thrilled his uncle knew of the special care he had been giving the beloved motorcycle and he promised to continue with this tradition until he, too, could pass it along to the next generation.

⁊ᘓ ⑭

I'm brushing my teeth right now. You can see that, right?
Standing alone in my bathroom, I was talking to the

large mirror hanging above the sink. With a mouthful of toothpaste and suds foaming like an overflowing washing machine, I paused and listened. I could sense a nonphysical presence standing to my left—a woman. This surprised me, and I felt slightly unsettled. How was she able to connect with me here at home? Not to mention follow me into the bathroom, for crying out loud.

I have very well-developed psychic and energetic muscles, and I maintain strict rules regarding boundaries. Spirits, souls, entities, ghosts, aliens, and any other nonphysical beings do not get to talk with me when I'm off the clock, nor are they allowed into my home or personal life without invitation. I maintain this level of psychic hygiene to protect the work, my clients, and myself. This enables me to sustain a high level of intensity, focus, and clarity during sessions. If I brought my work home with me, it would be easy to burn out and become depleted, or even sick. Then I'm no help to anyone, whether at work or with my own family and friends.

Yet even this level of rigor has its occasional blind spots and loopholes. And, as crazy as it sounds, brushing my teeth has a tendency to swing the psychic door wide open. This was not the first time I found myself visited by something or someone out of the ordinary during my morning routine.

I believe these visitations are possible due to a unique combination of circumstances. I'm usually zoned out, as brushing my teeth does not require active attention.

Therefore, my brain can shift into a slightly altered state of nonfocus. Also, the brushing motion provides a rhythm which my body registers tactically and audibly, thus deepening relaxation and prompting a brain wave state which elicits psychic awareness. Finally, the mirror and the water boost the conductivity of environmental energies. Tap water, while not as strong a conductor as sea water, still boosts reception and transmission of energy. This might explain why a lot of us experience genius moments while taking a shower. Almost everyone has come up with an amazing new idea or downloaded the perfect solution to a problem during their morning shower.

Mirrors have long been considered portals to other realms. It's all about perspective, though, my guides remind me. If you're open to it, a mirror can act like a lens focusing mental energies and intention outward to other dimensions and sentient beings, or inward bringing communication and information to you. Mirrors, like any objects, are not active on their own; they become active with our attention, focus, and intent. Those on the other side can use mirrors in the same way we do to boost communication and access additional information.

"Tell my daughter that I am still here. She is so sad," the woman said telepathically.

With a mouthful of minty foam, I set the toothbrush down. She had my full attention now. I opened my mind and began focusing on her energy with a deliberate intention to learn more. I became aware that she was talking about a new client I would be seeing at my office later in the day—a daughter who was grieving the loss of her mother. However, her mother was still alive! What an unexpected detail. How was this possible?

This happens sometimes, although it is rare. When a living person's mind becomes fragmented and unfocused due to illness, trauma, substance abuse, or coma, psychic dimensions can become more easily accessible. They might find themselves entering the same nonphysical realms visited by spirits, the deceased, and mediums. The more frequently the dissociated living person visits these states, the easier it is for others who are sensitive (like me) to hear, see, or feel them.

In this case, my loving and concerned nonphysical visitor was living with Alzheimer's disease in her physical body, and it had progressed to a stage where her brain was unable to keep her focused in ordinary reality. Her daughter, and any others who loved and cared for her, would likely observe this as a decrease in her ability to communicate and respond to her physical environment. For the mother, however, this dissociation freed her consciousness to inhabit and communicate from nonordinary dimensions. *Fascinating and heartbreaking, all at once,* I thought.

How can I help? I offered mentally.

"First of all, please reassure her that I haven't gone anywhere. I am still with her and love her with all my heart. That will never change. Next, I want to let her know that she and I can learn to communicate this way, psychically and telepathically."

She was articulate and it was easy for me to connect with her intelligence energetically. The intensity of her love fueled a strong desire to maintain contact with her daughter. And as the disease progressed, her consciousness was adapting to become more creative and powerful. This made sense to me. She was essentially accomplishing what you or I might when expanding our own conscious awareness through mindfulness practices and meditation. I realized the mother must also possess natural psychic abilities, otherwise I would not be able to perceive her so clearly. From a medical intuitive perspective, I wondered if the damage occurring in her brain was breaking down built-in inhibitions. If she was no longer tethered to the neurobiological processes which govern a conventional relationship to time and space, was she now psychically free to travel and communicate outside of the usual parameters?

I promised that my guides and I would do anything possible on our end to share her message and facilitate this next chapter in their relationship. This was not going to get any easier for them at the human, day-to-day level. However, with Spirit's help, they could forge new bonds and methods of relating that promised to be just as rewarding.

Later that day, when it came time to meet my new client, I felt like I already knew her. She appeared fragile, almost defeated. Her eyes were large and brimming with unshed tears. I wanted to hug her and tell her that her mom was okay, more than okay; she was vital, present, and strong. I waited, however, knowing that I needed to follow the usual protocol for opening a psychic reading. It wasn't my place to tell her these things, at least not right away. Her mother, the family's spirit guides, and the wisdom of our higher selves would do most of the talking. I was to be a clear, neutral channel, delivering healing words and love in a way that would best serve my client and her family. And, as always, I was determined to do the best job I could.

Once the session was formally underway, the daughter listened intently to the information I relayed from her mother. As each minute passed, I sensed my client becoming increasingly calm and peaceful, as if her entire being could finally breathe an enormous sigh of relief. She shared that hearing from her mother in this way made her realize they would never lose each other, no matter what was to come. Her mother was still her mother in all ways that are important, and she would learn to develop and trust this new and special way of relating.

Chapter Ten

N*ever read a reader,* I thought to myself, amused, slouching down in my seat. I hoped this would make me magically invisible to the man onstage. Too late, unfortunately. He already had me pegged and I knew exactly what was coming next.

"I see the image of a man—quite handsome, actually. He's waving both arms trying to get my attention," he announced into the microphone in his hand. "He is someone's father . . . I sense he may have passed from suicide." The audience, seated in the dark, gasped audibly within the cavernous space of a famously haunted 1850s building in Seattle's Pioneer Square.

Dammit, Dad, please stop talking to the psychic, I mentally cried out. *He's going to come over here if you don't!* Right on cue, the psychic turned, aiming his mic like a radar antenna, homing in on my exact position in the audience.

"Your dad has passed?" he asked while making his way toward me.

"Yes," I mumbled, looking down. *I really don't want to do this,* I thought, *not here, in front of all these people.* It was a full house at the invitation-only demonstration featuring the well-known psychic medium. I had been looking forward to this evening; however, I wanted to be an anonymous face in the crowd rather than an audience participant.

Suddenly, the psychic laughed out loud, causing confused murmuring to ripple through the large gathering. He said with a smile, "Your dad tells me you wish I would have ignored him and walked right on by."

Yes, I wanted to reply, *that's true because my dad knows I can already hear him just fine without your assistance.* I couldn't help laughing though and nodded in agreement. *Okay then, let's see where this goes,* I thought.

The psychic took a deep breath, crossing his arms while still managing the mic in his hand, "There's another man here too, and I'm sorry to say he's telling me that he died by his own hand as well. I'm wondering if they are related somehow." He paused for a moment, then continued. Your father says they are a group or something?" The psychic's eyes widen in surprise. "I've just heard 'call us the Suicide

Club.' Does that make sense to you?"

All I could say was, "Yes."

I heard a loud whisper from a few seats away. "Oh that poor woman, how tragic."

My eyes began to fill with tears, though I wasn't sad. I felt frustrated because I consider myself fortunate and blessed, and far from pitiable. I was also feeling overflowing love and pride, because I understood clearly what the psychic was picking up on. My father works with others in the spirit world who have also died by suicide, assisting them as they make their transition.

The person next to me politely offered a tissue. As I wiped my eyes, the psychic's focus shifted to communicating messages of love from my father and how much joy it brings him to see how our family has grown. Even though I already knew this through my own intuitive sense, it was lovely to hear anyway. My heart felt warm and happy as the psychic moved on to the next audience member who would be receiving a message from Spirit that night.

෨෬

Forgiveness and understanding are processes, not destinations. Allowing the journey to unfold organically—in its own way and time—is a beautiful gift of self-care and self-love. I believe the Creative Force we spring from wants us to love ourselves deeply so we may then extend that love to others, allowing them their own unique unfoldment. Love reminds us that within the other, we will always find ourselves.

After death, Dad realized his life was not over. He learned that his role in our family was not the villain (as he had come to believe). Rather, it was the teacher and healer. His words and actions, painful as they were, launched each member of our family onto deeply personal and profound healing trajectories that would continue for decades, if not generations. In order to evolve beyond the trauma of his passing, he was given the opportunity to remain available to all of us, whether it was consciously, as in my case as a psychic medium, or otherwise (dream visitation or synchronicities). We could continue to grow and heal as a family, with his help.

I remember my father as he was when he was still with us in the physical world, although it feels like lifetimes ago. We have both matured emotionally and spiritually over the ensuing years and now our relationship is light-years beyond what it was as parent and child. Who would have ever guessed that we would be coworkers? If a client session has to do with family issues related to depression, addiction, or suicide, Dad will often be present as a helping guide. He also acts as a sort of spiritual technician and communication specialist. When a departed loved one wants to get through to a client, he will offer them direction regarding the best way to communicate with me so that I can relay the message as accurately as possible. He might also help boost the vibrational signal so that I receive information more clearly. Another one of his gifts is bringing humor into a session when a dose of fresh perspective is most needed.

It is worth staying open to the possibility that all is not lost when circumstances would have you believe otherwise. A last goodbye is not always final. There is so much more to the story when we see death as a continuation rather than a conclusion.

Chapter Eleven

The summer sun came through my office doorway embodied in the radiant, beaming smile of a six-month-old baby boy. Although this was my first time ever seeing him, I already knew him well. I was used to his brilliant energy, as we had met many times before he was born. And here he was at last—as he always said he would be—held in the arms of his mother.

She and I had been meeting in sessions for years. Our work together encompassed energy healing with shamanic medicine and insight into expanding both her business and personal life with information from psychic reading work and spiritual counseling. She was deeply committed to her spiritual practice and energetic well-being, and it showed in her warm heart, clear mind, and healthy body.

Although, what she desired more than anything else was a true romantic partner, someone with whom she could share her life and raise a family. During the psychic reading portion of her visits, I could easily see that it was in her soul's plan to meet this partner and have children. Indeed, many times, the information I received about her future husband was quite detailed, right down to his hair color, military background, and business ownership.

And then, unexpectedly, another male began to make his presence telepathically known to me. His energy was strong and direct, and it made my eyes tear up to feel the boundless love he felt for my client. His intention was crystal clear—he was the soul of her future son and he wanted her to know, beyond any doubt, that he would be coming one day. Naturally, this news thrilled my client, and her eyes lit up as I shared the message. She felt ready, beyond ready, to meet this special romantic partner and to be a devoted mother. The readings suggested this would happen soon.

Some time passed. And then more time passed. In fact, a year went by and she had still not met her partner. Why would the Universe affirm her desires and then fail to deliver? Was she doing something wrong? Had she somehow missed her opportunity for love and happiness? These questions plagued her, and she grew increasingly disappointed and disheartened. Yet the messages in her sessions were always reassuring and reminded her that the visions she held in her heart for love and motherhood would be fulfilled. She must keep her heart open.

I felt torn. As a practitioner, I had long ago learned to trust the messages that came from Spirit. In addition, I had great confidence in my own trained psychic senses. I had no doubt that her positive future outcome would come to fruition. Yet as a woman, my heart went out to her and I could relate to her feelings of frustration and heartache. I, too, wondered why was it taking so long. Why did her psychic readings suggest a certain timeline that wasn't panning out in her human experience?

Fortune-telling, forecasting, and predictions are extraordinarily difficult aspects of psychic work. Many psychics and mediums will not offer these specific services, and I understand why. Reading an infinite amount of probable outcomes with any accuracy is a colossal task that requires masterful psychic abilities and phenomenal focus. As a psychic, it is vital to understand, and be comfortable with, the paradox that free will and destiny work closely together. These aspects are not opposites so much as complementary cosmic fundamentals of manifestation. Yes, we have free will and can walk outside and make any number of choices that will alter our futures. And, yes, there is also a plan, a blueprint, managing the trajectory of our lives. How can both be true?

Both are true because the Universe is multidimensional, not dualistic, as most of us have been trained to accept. We human beings rigorously declare something is either right or wrong; it cannot be both. The Universe seemingly agrees and then adds a twist at the last moment: yes, you are absolutely right; yet, this thing over here is right also, and that choice over there is right, too. It is a matter of Creative perspective, and from where the Universe is sitting, it is *all* right. Everything is correct, and nothing is wrong.

I know that this sounds like some kind of convenient spin story—the Universe and your friendly neighborhood psychic conspiring to hedge their bets. If, just for a moment, you expand your perspective and think like the Creation-descended artist you are, then you can get a sense of how this works. Your life is your biggest work of art. You choose the design, the composition, and the colors. There is no such thing as right or wrong in art; it is all simply art. You are free to appreciate it or not, like it or not, buy it or not. However, none of these choices render the art true or false.

So, how does this relate to my client? Well, let us go a little deeper. Creating in this reality entails one other vital consideration: co-creation. We do not dance on this world stage alone. It takes two to tango, as the saying goes. And we begin tangoing with our love partner in a quantum entanglement sort of way long before we ever meet them in person. Two souls, two focuses of Creative intention, become attracted to one another before they are born into a physical body. Once earthside, even though they may be far apart from one another in space or time, they are still interacting with, and impacting, the other.

How and why does this happen? This occurs for many reasons that are deeply personal to each individual. Sometimes, these two souls are continuing corporeal stories that began many chapters (lifetimes) ago and circumstances have once again become conducive to the expansion of previous narratives. Other times, these souls may be looking for a respite or recess from ongoing reincarnational stories and will choose a partner for play or ease. Some hardier souls—like the friend you know who parachutes out of airplanes—will decide to veer off into a risky relationship, seeking thrills or an adrenaline rush.

In each one of these cases, the axiom of co-creation still applies. This means that either or both souls can make choices in their respective environments that hinder or delay syncing up with their intended love. Free will of the individual human consciousness collaborates with the higher soul self and its intentions. What might this look like through the eyes of your ego? It might look like failure. It might look like your beloved is never coming.

All of this is a psychic reader's nightmare. It is absolutely the hardest part of my job. When a client is feeling pain, all the cosmic considerations and explanations I might offer are cold comfort. I know this and yet, as much as I might wish to, I cannot change how the Universe operates.

Happily, in the end, my client did meet her beloved partner. His hair color, background, and profession were, indeed, what her reading had foretold. And they had a son, whose smile shone like the summer sun the day I finally got to meet him in my office.

ಬೆ ಲ

I talk to a lot of babies before they are born. A lot. They are very wise and often very chatty. Many times, they are the first presence I pick up on during a psychic reading. They barrel through my office door (energetically speaking), cutting in front of my client, ready to take the session over. And they really are terrific spokespeople (spokes-souls?) and highly invested in helping my client because, well, my client is about to become one of their parents.

I enjoy working with these souls who are on their way to becoming someone's child, because they occupy a unique plane of existence that is easy to access psychically. Unlike some of the other realms where souls spend their nonearthly existence, this particular plane is uniquely earthbound, a type of platform situated right next to us that offers a direct gateway into our world.

For me, it is a great joy when a client brings their newborn into the office and I finally get to gaze upon the face of the soul I have already come to know so well. I have found over the years that souls become almost more real to me than the people they inhabit. Because I can connect fully and deeply with those on the other side, these disembodied relationships become very real and meaningful. They become just as important as the relationships I have with my fellow human beings. In many ways, those soul connections I make during a session can be more profound because our human filters don't get in the way. The soul and I connect and interact purely without pretense, appearances, withholding, or any of the myriad ways we humans get snagged in our interactions with each other. The nonphysical soul and I are free to interact and enjoy the gift of connection. There are no attachments or expectations.

Often the incoming soul wants to reassure the future parent that they are working together, and the baby wants to come just as much as the parent, or parents, want them to. We forget, sometimes, that we don't have to do all of this alone as parents-to-be. The family forms long before the baby arrives.

The role of a baby's gender is an interesting one from the perspective of the soul. Understandably, parents are curious about the sex of their baby. Usually, I am shown this psychically even before the parent asks. I strive to be tactful and considerate about this information, however, since not everyone wants to know beforehand. I have learned through these kinds of sessions that souls consider the selection of gender and sexuality to be creative expressions and learning tools.

Some souls are clear about these choices from the beginning. And, yes, it does appear to be a choice made between the aspect of the soul preparing to incarnate and the larger soul self, or higher self. I have not yet been told or shown that there is one God dictating choice or appropriateness of any particular gender expression or choice of sexuality. From the Universal perspective, it appears that we experience many facets and combinations over many different lifetimes. The ultimate goal is to understand the various perspectives humanity provides, such as race, intelligence, affluence, and religion. Perspectives that are, perhaps, difficult for us to comprehend in our experience while living in this literal world of black and white, right and wrong.

From the perspective of the soon-to-be baby, life is an exciting proposition, even when the soul who is arriving knows it is committing to an experience filled with serious mental, physical, or environmental challenges. Most, if not all, of these challenges are planned and known about ahead of time, with some of the most profound having been discussed and agreed upon before the parents or even grandparents were born.

Ancestral stories are one of the main frameworks souls use to learn and grow during a human lifetime. Each lifetime can represent one chapter in a grand, ongoing, thematic story encompassing an entire family of souls. Consider your own family this lifetime—whether the one you're born into, the one you're brought into, or the one you choose yourself—and it is easy to see the extraordinary potential each member has for being the source of your greatest joy or your greatest sorrow.

Unborn siblings also play a big role in psychic readings. A lot of laughing has erupted during readings when I convey to the client—who may not even have any children yet—that her two future children are already bickering about who "gets to go first." Even though soul plans are known ahead of time, last minute changes can be made if necessary for the benefit of all. A great example of this is—hold onto your hats—a gender switch.

I remember a reading where the soul said to me, "I don't know. I'll probably be a boy. Although I'm considering being a girl, a very strong-willed and opinionated girl. That would give my dad a real challenge and that's a big reason why I'm coming into the family, to turn the balance of power upside down." And then she laughed with humor, love, and anticipation. *Oh boy (or girl!), these parents have their work cut out for them,* I thought to myself.

I have been in practice long enough now that some of these beautiful souls who made their debut during a psychic reading—years before they were born—are entering high school. It always makes me smile when a proud parent scrolls through their cell phone to show me the latest family photo. Little do they know a future *grandchild* may be in the room with us, peeking over their shoulders . . . but I'm getting ahead of myself . . .

Conclusion

You may—or may not—have noticed the dedication at the front of this book. Some of you might be like me and read the entire front matter of a book, including the introduction, table of contents, and dedication. I even read the copyright and Library of Congress cataloguing data. Others of you may prefer to just get on with it and go straight to the first chapter. And, steel yourself, I am aware of at least one human currently walking among us who makes a habit of reading the *final* page of a book *first*. This makes my brain wince like running fingernails across a chalkboard. (You know who you are and it's a good thing we grew to love you long before we learned this about you.)

So that you don't have to shuffle the pages back to the front of this book, here is what the dedication said:

For Jim
1945–2018

You knew what it meant.
For that, and everything else, my love and eternal thanks.

Everyone needs to be seen. Everyone needs someone who believes in them. Jim was my someone. His students, patients, and colleagues knew him as an accomplished and beloved psychologist and professor. I knew him differently—personally—and this how I learned he was, in his heart, a poet. He understood what it meant to dedicate your life in service to something far greater than yourself. He saw in me a similar dedication and knew, before I did, that my life would never be the same and there would be no going back. He reminded me to proceed with love, grace, patience and, whenever possible, a sense of humor.

Sometimes we are invited to walk a path that veers from the ordinary ways. We transcend convention when we follow our inspiration to seek out what is around the evolutionary bend. Some of us are pioneers and find our seeking leads to a somewhat solitary existence. Not everyone wants to go where we are going, or learn what we are learning.

106

Sometimes we have to say goodbye to those who ask us to stay small so that they may feel safe in our presence. If you ever find yourself in this position, I encourage you to send out a prayer asking for your own Jim. Until then, please know that I am here, and I see you, with love always.

It seems a long time ago now. I was driving home from my shamanic practitioner graduation ceremony. The day commemorated and celebrated the culmination of the previous six years of my life, and every single drop of blood, sweat, and tears I had shed along the way. Two dozen of us stood in a circle while our wise and cherished teacher bestowed our practitioner certificates.

It was late afternoon and the springtime sun cast long rays across the lanes of blacktop freeway. In the back seat, my baskets—made of reeds and grasses—were lined up, each holding carefully packed shamanic medicine tools: rattles, feathered prayer fans, cast bronze bells, braids of sweetgrass, and an abalone shell cupping dried sprigs of white sage. Nestled on the floorboard, wrapped in criss-crossing fabric layers of colorful Balinese prayer shawls, lay a shaman's drum, as precious to me as the rarest jewel. These objects represented a blending of hundreds of cultures whose healing traditions have traversed continents and oceans for millennia.

The tools of my new trade.

No, trade was definitely not the correct word. Service,

was that the word? The tools of my new service? No, that was still not quite right.

Then I heard it, of course. The voice that had been guiding me all along, from my very first memory.

"Meaghan, you have answered the call. Welcome. There is much to do, let us begin."

Yes, I thought, this is it. The calling. I am ready.

About the Author

Meaghan O'Leary, MDiv, PhD, is a psychic medium and spiritual advisor. She is a certified practitioner of both shamanic energy medicine and past life regression therapy. Practicing in Seattle since 2002, she serves clients and students worldwide with psychic intuitive readings, transpersonal spiritual counseling, shamanic healing and ceremony, and past life/between life hypnotherapy.

When she is not gallivanting across spiritual and cosmic dimensions, Meaghan enjoys the beaches, mountains, and forests of her home in the Pacific Northwest. She is an avid traveler appreciating art, architecture, history, and cultures (and a bit of ghost hunting) across the globe.

For more information, please visit *meaghanoleary.com*.

Made in the USA
Columbia, SC
18 February 2020

88028715R00079